The Spelling Game by R.J. Westwell

The Spelling Game

improving the working memory and vocabulary

by Dr Rosemary Westwell

Spelling!

Memory!

Vocabulary!

The Spelling Game by R.J. Westwell

The Spelling Game that improves the working memory and increases vocabulary.

We know that our language is stored in our brains according to the sounds of the words. (Thus, when we are recalling language, we often make mistakes and recall the wrong word – one that sounds very similar to the one intended.)

Learners often have difficulty in retaining information in the working memory for any length of time. In addition, at first, the information that they can store is very limited.

This game is designed to take note of and address these matters. Words that sound similar and contain similar patterns are grouped together. Pictures are used to interrupt the recalling process and to engage the learner in another activity before producing the word(s) being learnt thereby forcing the student to retain the word(s) in his/her working memory for a longer time than usual. The pages are designed to be used flexibly. Learners can gradually increase the amount of information they try to retain in their working memory until they can measure their success by remembering up to 56 words at a time.

This game is ideal for pair work and involves only supervision on the part of the teacher.

The Spelling Game by R.J. Westwell

Before you play:

You may wish to teach the following 'spelling rules':

1. 'i' before 'e' except after 'c'

2. a, e, i, o, u as in 'cap', 'bed', 'it', 'on', 'us' (short vowels)

add 'e' and they become:

ae, ee, ie, oe, ue as in 'cape', 'been', 'bite', 'bone', 'use' (long vowels)

3. when adding '-ed':

with long vowels there is one consonant in the middle e.g. 'boned'

with short vowels, the consonant is doubled e.g. capped

4. to add '–ing', drop the 'e'

.e.g. make – making

5. to add 'y' at the end of a word:

   2 consonants before, keep the 'e' as in donkey

   1 consonant before, drop the 'e' as in shaky

The Spelling Game by R.J. Westwell

More spelling rules:

6. double the 'll' when full is alone

   Take away an 'l' when 'ful' is at the end

as in "He was full of thanks - he was thankful."

7. - tion has a vowel before (as in station)

   -sion does not (as in mansion)

e.g. nation, pension

8. ante with 'e' = before, anti with 'i' = against

e.g. anteroom, antenatal

   anticlimax. anticlockwise, antifreeze

9. 'c' with 'k' is 'c' (pronounced 'k') as in pack

   'c' on its own is 'c' (pronounced 's') as in pace

10. -cious, -tious have a vowel before (as in precious and cautious)

   -scious does not (as in conscious)

e.g. vicious, cautious, audacious, fictitious, officious, judicious, unconscious

The Spelling Game by R.J. Westwell

How to play:

Student A and B look at a group of seven words, describe patterns and notable features and check the meanings.

e.g.

1. 'watch', wad, waffle …' contain the letter 'a' that is pronounced like 'o' as in 'pot'. 'Watch' has a silent 't'.

Student A (with the help of student B) **while trying to remember how to spell the word**, associates each word with a picture by creating a sentence (or two) that contain(s) the focus word.

e.g. picture A1 is a picture of a bathroom. The sentence(s) could be 'We should **watch** how much water we use in the bathroom. It could be too much.'

Student A finishes making up sentences that relate each word to each picture on the rest of the sheet.

Student B takes away the word sheet while student A looks at the pictures and writes down the list of words from memory. Students B checks student 'A's answers.

Roles are reversed.

Dr R. J. Westwell

The Spelling Game by R.J. Westwell

CONTENTS

The following page is a 'contents page' that contains the list of letter patterns contained in this book. It can easily be added to for the needs of you students!

The Spelling Game by R.J. Westwell

1) as in wash
2) –able
3) acqu
4) ad
5) ad-
6) ad-
7) ad-
8) add
9) ae (aeroplane)
10) af
11) aff
12) -ai
13) -al
14) al-
15) -all
16) am-
17) –amm-
18) ap-
19) app-
20) ar-
21) -ar
22) arr-
23) -ary
24) as-
25) ass
26) au-
27) -au-
28) aw (draw)
29) -ay
30) silent b (numb)
31) c (centre)
32) ch (ache)
33) -ci (official)
34) -ck
35) –ei-
36) e (made)
37) ea (health)
38) el
39) –ell
40) -er
41) -ery (mastery)
42) fl-
43) -fle
44) fr-
45) -ge
46) -gh (enough)
47) -gle
48) -gue
49) i (onion)
50) -ic
51) le-
52) i-e
53) ie (ladies)
54) ie (quiet)
55) -igh
56) ir-
57) j (jar)
58) k-
59) il-
60) -il
61) -imm
62) –inn-
63) o (won)
64) o (amoeba)
65) -oa
66) o-e
67) oi-
68) –or (actor)
69) or (fork)
70) –ore (more)
71) -ory
72) –ou- (ought)
73) –our (flour)
74) -our (colour)
75) ow (cow)
76) -oy
77) –p-
78) –pp-
79) ph
80) –qu-
81) –rr-
82) -ss
83) -sion (vision)
84) -ssion
85) -stle
86) –tt-
87) th (thin)
88) thr
89) –ti- (partial)
90) u (union)
91) -tion
92) -ure
93) wa (walk)
94) wh-
95) wr-
96) -zz

The Spelling Game by R.J. Westwell

1. a as in watch
watch
wad
waffle
wander
was
what
wash

2. –able
able
admirable
agreeable
amenable
curable
delectable
durable

3. acqu-
acquaint
acquaintance
acquiescence
acquire
acquisition
acquit
acquittal

4. ad
adamant
adapt
adept
adhere
adhesion
adhesive
admonish

5. ad-
adjective
adjoin
adjudicate
adjust
administer
admirable
admit

6. ad-
admire
adolescent
adventure
adverb
adverse
advice
advise

7. ad-
adopt
adore
adrift
adroit
adult
advertise
advertisement

8. add
add
adder
addict
addition
address
advance
advantage

9. ae- (aeroplane)
aerial
aerobics
aerodynamics
aeronaut
aeroplane
aerosol
aesthetic

10. af-
afar
afraid
afresh
aft
after
afternoon
afterwards

11. aff-
affable
affection
affix
afflict
afford
affordable
affray

12. –ai
ascertain
Britain
certain
mountain
obtain
refrain
sprain

The Spelling Game by R.J. Westwell

A1

A2

A3

A4

A5

A6

A7

The Spelling Game by R.J. Westwell

13. –al
crystal
equal
filial
final
minimal
naval
viral

14. al-
albatross
algebra
alimentary
alimony
alpine
altruism
always

15. –all
all
ball
basketball
call
callfootfall
cannonball
wall

16. . am-
amateur
amaze
amen
amicable
amnesia
amount
amuse

17. -amm-
clammy
grammar
hammer
jamming
rammed
stammer
stammered

18. ap-
apart
apartment
apathetic
ape
aperitif
aperture
apt

19. app-
appal
appeal
appease
apple
appreciate
apprise
approve

20. ar-
arbitrary
arc
arched
ardent
arduous
argument
arsenal

21. –ar
familiar
peculiar
pillar
popular
regular
scholar
vinegar

22. arr-
arrange
array
arrears
arrest
arrival
arrogance
arrow

23. –ary
binary
contrary
customary
February
January
necessary
ordinary

24. as-
ascend
aspect
aspersion
asphyxia
aspiration
astonishment
astound

The Spelling Game by R.J. Westwell

B!

B2

B3

B4

B5

B6

B7

The Spelling Game by R.J. Westwell

25. ass-
assassinate
assault
assemble
assertion
assertive
assessment
assignment

26. au-
audience
aural
authentic
autobiography
autograph
automatic
automobile

27. –au-
caught
daughter
fraudulent
fraught
gaunt
haunt
jaunty

28. aw (draw)
awful
awkward
bawling
claw
drawing
hawking
lawyer

29. ay
affray
array
crayfish
dray
mayor
prayer
prayerful

30. silent b (numb)
aplomb
bomb
climb
comb
crumb
dumb
lamb

31. c (centre)
cement
cemetery
cenotaph
censor
cent
certificate
cessation

32. ch (ache)
archaeology
chemical
chemistry
orchestra
scheme
scholar
school

33. -ci (official)
artificial
commercial
crucial
facial
financial
social
special

34. –ck
acknowledge
awestruck
chickpea
chopstick
chuckle
crackle
cricket

35. –ei-
abseil
ageism
beige
caffeine
conceited
deceitful
receive

36. e (made)
apex
caged
fade
flame
jade
shame
waded

The Spelling Game by R.J. Westwell

C1

C2

C3

C4

C5

C6

C7

The Spelling Game by R.J. Westwell

37. ea (health)	41. -ery (mastery)	45. –ge
stealth	finery	baggage
health	gallery	bandage
bread	misery	cabbage
dread	mystery	camouflage
breath	nunnery	carnage
death	query	garbage
wealth	tannery	wattage

38. –el	42. fl-	46. -gh (enough)
camel	flabby	cough
channel	flavour	draught
funnel	fledgling	enough
marvel	fluffy	laughter
pastel	flurry	rough
quarrel	fluster	tough
tunnel	flutter	trough

39. –ell-	43. –fle	47. –gle
bellows	baffle	bangle
cellulose	raffle	bugle
cowbell	rifle	dangle
felling	ruffle	dingle
marvellous	stifle	entangle
travelling	trifle	mingle
yelling	waffle	wangle

40. –er	44. fr-	48. –gue
barber	fracas	ague
caterer	fragile	argue
jotter	framing	catalogue
leather	frayed	epilogue
master	frenetic	fatigue
paper	frightening	fugue
pepper	frigid	intrigue

The Spelling Game by R.J. Westwell

D1

D2

D3

D4

D5

D6

D7

The Spelling Game by R.J. Westwell

49. i (onion)	53. ie as in ladies	57. j (jar)
billion	analogies	jailor
bunion	bier	jasmine
companion	birdie	jaws
million	budgies	jest
opinion	calorie	jostle
pillion	maladies	judge
union	parodies	justice

50. –ic	54. ie as in quiet	58. k-
chronic	clients	khaki
euphoric	crier	kitchen
exotic	diet	kennel
fantastic	dietician	kid
hypnotic	fiery	kindness
stoic	flier	kaftans
toxic	science	kaleidoscope

51. ie-	55. –igh	59. il-
achieve	alight	illegal
aggrieved	fight	illegible
believe	flight	illiterate
brief	height	illusion
irretrievable	plight	illusive
mischievous	sigh	illustration
reprieve	tight	illustrious

52. i-e	56. ir-	60. –il
appetite	irascible	basil
coincide	irate	council
despite	iridescent	daffodil
dynamite	iris	devil
maritime	irksome	distil
suicide	iron	fulfil
undermine	ironic	instil

The Spelling Game by R.J. Westwell

E1

E2

E3

E4

E5

E6

E7

The Spelling Game by R.J. Westwell

61. imm-
immaculate
immature
immeasurable
immerse
immersion
immobile
immune

62. –inn-
beginning
cinnamon
dinner
grinning
thinned
whinny
winnings

63. o (won)
does
honey
money
once
one
won
wonderful

64. oe (amoeba)
amoeba
apnoea
diarrhoea
oesophagus
oestrogen
onomatopoeia
phoebe

65. –oa
afloat
approach
charcoal
cloakroom
coastal
cocoa
hoax

66. o-e
alcove
backbone
clone
cope
elope
phone
telescope

67. oi
android
avoidance
boisterous
embroider
choice
moisten
noise

68. -or (actor)
manor
mayor
juror
advisor
alligator
anchor
exterior

69. –or- (fork)
abhor
borderline
bored
cordial
corkscrew
dormitory
north

70. –ore (more)
aforethought
beforehand
boredom
carnivore
deplore
explore
eyesore

71. –ory
accessory
advisory
cursory
dormitory
factory
history
story

72. –ou- (ought)
afterthought
bought
brought
dour
fought
ought
thought

The Spelling Game by R.J. Westwell

F1

F3

F2

F4

F5

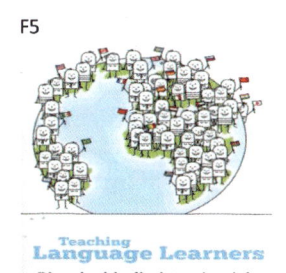

F6

F7

The Spelling Game by R.J. Westwell

73. –our (flour)
abound
expound
flour
flouted
foundation
gouge
spouse

74. -our (colour)
ardour
armour
colour
flavour
honour
humour
labour

75. ow (cow)
allowance
brown
cowardice
crowning
flower
howl
powder

76. –oy
annoy
buoy
choirboy
decoy
destroy
employ
enjoy

77. –p-
apartment
apathy
aperture
apology
epiglottis
opening
upended

78. –pp-
appalled
apparatus
apparently
appealing
application
appreciate
apprehension

79. ph
photogenic
graphic
alphabet
amphibian
apostrophe
atmosphere
autograph

80. –qu-
acquaintance
acquire
aquatic
barbeque
cheque
equality
quarter

81. –rr-
barrow
carry
irrefutable
married
merry
quarry
starred

82. –ss (mass)
assassin
cessation
essential
fitness
happiness
messiness
pessimistic

83. -sion (vision)
concision
confusion
derision
fusion
Illusion
lesion
revision

84. –ssion
aggression
compassion
depression
expression
mission
passion
profession

The Spelling Game by R.J. Westwell

G1

G2

G3

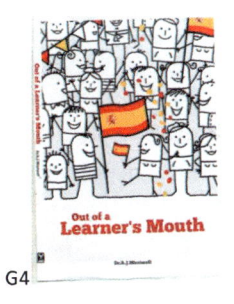

G4

G5

G6

G7

The Spelling Game by R.J. Westwell

85. –stle
bristle
bustle
castle
hastle
jostle
thistle
whistle

86. –tt-
bitterly
blotter
butter
letter
matter
pattern
twittering

87. th (thin)
death
ether
filth
theory
thief
think
thorough

88. thr
arthritis
enthralled
thread
thrifty
throbbing
throw
thrust

89. –ti- (partial)
circumstantial
confidential
credential
impartial
initial
potential
spatial

90. u (union)
abuse
acumen
annual
argue
impunity
unity
usual

91. –tion
addition
edition
equation
flotation
nation
petition
subtraction

92. –ure
aperture
furniture
manicure
nature
picture
rapture
rupture

93. wa (walk)
award
walked
warble
warm
warning
warped
water

94. wh-
wheat
whereabouts
whereas
whether
whinge
who
whose

95. wr-
wreath
wrestle
wriggle
writhing
writing
wrong
wrought

96. –zz
bedazzle
blizzard
dazzling
fizzling
frizzle
jazz
sizzle

The Spelling Game by R.J. Westwell

H1

H2

H3

H4

H5

H6

H7

The Spelling Game by R.J. Westwell

This method may be applied to a variety of other materials and information. The author has successfully used it with memorising poetry, names of people and musical terms and phrases.

For more information please feel welcome to contact the author:

Dr. R.J.Westwell (PhD, MA TESOL, MA Ed, B Mus, BA Hons)

 rjwestwell@hotmail.com; rjwestwell1@yahoo.com

PhD thesis "The development of language acquisition in a mature learner" : http://eprints.ioe.ac.uk/48/

www.reviewsrjs.wordpress.com; www.elyforlanguage.wordpress.com

books:

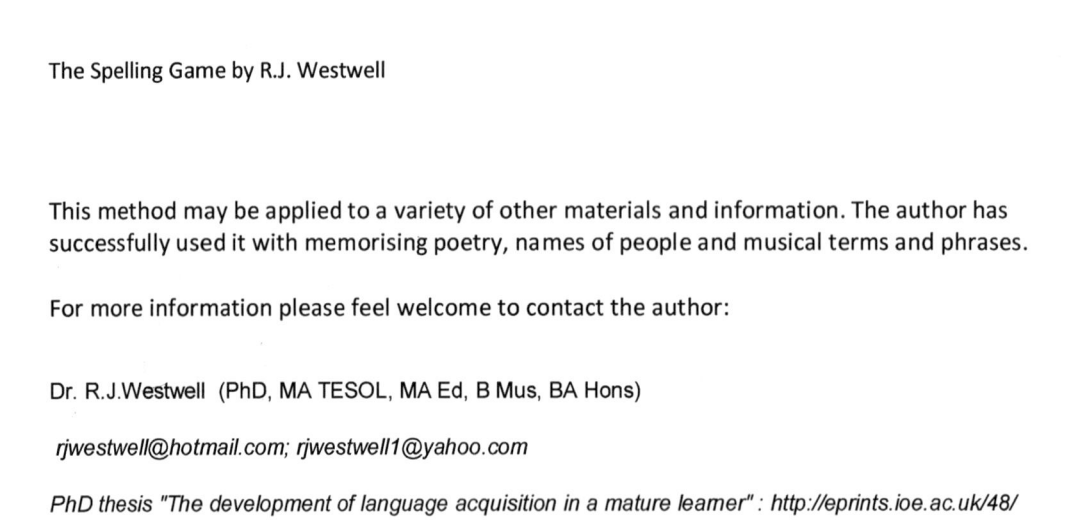

'Out of a Learners' Mouth' (the trials and tribulations of learning Spanish as a mature beginner) (Burrows Ely www.burrowsbookshop.co.uk)

'Teaching Language Learners' a book of ideas for teaching EFL (Cambridge International Book Centre www.eflbooks.co.uk)

'John, Dementia and Me' a semi-autobiographical novel on early-onset dementia (North Staffordshire Press Ltd. malcolm.henson@editorial.staffs.com)

Printed in Great Britain
by Amazon.co.uk, Ltd.,
Marston Gate.